THE WAY

CHOOSE OR DON'T

B SRINIVAS CHAKRAVARTHI

Contents

Contents

Contents

Preface

PREFACE

This is Bommakanti Sriniva Chakravarthi. In short, you can call me, Vasu. My pen name is VasuBharat09. I am known to many a poetry lover all over the world with this name. I have so far brought out FOUR books. Among them, THREE are based on the poetry and One is with the short stories.

Just as the other three books, this book also deals with the poetry. Each poem in this book is titled with the word that is randomly picked up from the poem itself. Every time, it is not possible to name the poem, out and out, based on its gist. Hence, I plead you all not to connect the title with the gist of the poem.

When it comes to discuss the subject of this book, I can talk about it in short. If being soft or rough are considered the two aspects of life, it is up to One to decide to possess any one of these two or both. Strikingly, my book chooses the softness.

Accordingly, all the poems in this book are written so softly.

Thank you all and bless me.

Regards,

VASU,

Chapter1

AN UNBUILT PATH
An unbuilt path
I choose to tread.
It oscillates my way very often
but shows my life a straight one.
I walk on it in a dense forest being
away from the concrete jungle.
Earlier and now,
I am among the wild but
the difference is a lot more.
Formerly I heard
the deafening roars.

Chapter2

I fly here and there.
I know what my food is.
I earn it but don't gulp.
I fly back to my nest
and feed my chicks with it.
An eye on my chicks.
An eye on myself.
I don't fly far off.
I know who we are preys to.
I pin my faith in my eyes.
My eyes two are on predator.

Chapter3

COLORFUL WINGS
Hey, my cute soul,
where do you dwell, dear?
You seem flapping
your colourful wings
more than usual.
Must a bee have
cheered you up today or
must the rainbow in your disguise be
flying for a change?
Will you invite me to your palace as
I have a fistful of grains for our dinner.

Chapter4

PAINS
The pains behind
your smiles is a game,
an inevitable one,
that your life plays.
You are a self-esteem.
You have no other way.
The evaporating river
never exposes its tears
while those fly up.
Pains and tears
both of you hide.
I can't seek them but
can feel the ripples and smiles.

Chapter5

GIVER

Me, a giver.
I hide my strength
in the roots.
They hike my length
to your view.
Your attention I grab
making my fruits hang.
While I fight the Sun
you snore in my den.
I become your breaths
while you become breathless
to keep your oaths.
I root you deep.
Don't uproot me.

Chapter6

GREEN SKY
A tiny green sky
surprises me daily.
It moves unlike
the clouds move in a hurry.
How worthy its disposition is!
Prosperity it hides and says
I am there where I am.
A few days I shut the window.
I hear someone tap on it.
Its tender petals caress my cheeks.
It is not there where it was.

Chapter 7

SWEAT
Let my sweat flood
until my hunger
swims joyously.
Let the aches
of my labour echo
in the heart of Divine.
After all I am
eking out my livelihood.
Have no complaints against Him.
Mine is an obedient role.
Let it go. Otherwise,
My role remains vacant.

Chapter8

FLOOD

It drizzled the whole night.
I heard the tiny drops
slap my thatched roof.
Rain wrapped my mud
walls with a wet blanket.
The breeze kissed the walls
and hugged me causing chills.
To warm up my soul,
I raised the flame of the oil lamp
In the light, I saw
Nature's beauty flooding.

Chapter 9

WOMB
A womb of mother.
A womb of earth.
Where you start
there you halt.
It's a travel
with God's fuel.
So long as
breath fuels you,
you are alive.
So long as hunger
earns bread you survive.
Why do you make your life a hell?
In the blink of an eye,
life may shut its eye and
never open again.

Chapter 10

COAL DUST
Does the night smear her face
with the coal dust
to match it with her black gown?
How stunningly her beauty is!
The glitters of the stars and the moon
expose her charming complexion.
My drooping eyelids
seem tired of staring at her.
My snores sing melody while
serenity beats the drums.

Chapter11

A glance at you
hastily tattooed you on
my forehead.
I looked my face in the mirror
but I couldn't see you, so sad.
I realized I can't see
my fortune on the forehead.
I had a glance
at a bud as well yesterday.
It bloomed today.
It looked prettier than you.
My fortune is seen.

Chapter12

GRASS
I collect grass
or something else.
My efforts finally result
in shaping a pretty dwell.
The entrance has no doors.
You can any time have
an entry as well an exit for
I value life.
My heart is unlike my nest.
It is Divine's.
Never know its entrance.
Neve can have an exit.

Chapter13

SOLITARY

Though solitary,
I am not gloomy.
In the midnight,
what have I to do
on the shore?
I see many a falling,
However, glowing
star from the sky.
I hear the fuss of the falling rain or waves.
I realize the strength of the weak snow fall.
Is the ground their heaven where I am already?

Chapter14

WHISPERS
The whispers of
the whirlwinds can
never astound me.
The lightning of
the thunderbolts
can never light
my home lamps.
The cracks of the earthquake
can never break my glossy soul.
The glow of the fireflies can
never ignite my cool mind.
It is,
my love that might
shake my will.

Chapter15

LOVE CHILLS
My heart is looking for you
while my eyes are beating it.
My brain is penning
beautiful words while
my hands are thinking
how to welcome you.
My mind is nearing you while
my legs are becoming frozen.
My nose is helpless while
my mouth is breathing.
I am in chaos.

Chapter 16

BOAT
I made a boat
to wheel my life cycle.
From infancy to
dotage it has
to be paddled.
Hope is that
I can sail smoothly.
Hope is that
I can't achieve it.
Hope is strong
in either case.
Move man, move.
Or make it
your destination
where you start.

Chapter17

GESTURES

The gesture of love,
I receive from the trees,
rivers and mountains.
They hold neither a pen nor a sword.
Hence, the words remain unborn.
They get no provocation to look scorn.
Man's love utters,
hit or miss or do or die.
The love is dumb.
Its utterance is often silence.

Chapter18

CLOUDS

The running clouds
know that they
melt, rain and vanish.
Why does its
ephemeral life
make it rush and
whom does it favour?
When the lifeless
can run to favour man,
why does he
run to harm
his fellowmen?
When the lifeless can gain
immortality, Why not man?

Chapter 19

THE SUN
Has the Sun
learnt byheart the warmth
more than the heat these days?
Have the stones melted
and flowed inspiring the rivers?
Is an unnamed liquid
competing with water?
Is it love
that finally found its way?

Chapter20

I am not a sea like.
You can view my depth as
my heart is an abyss like.
You fly up and up
to touch the sky.
Water doesn't blanket me
as it blankets a sea.
Unless you fly down
you can't know me.
I resemble a nest.
You can call a halt
to your errands and rest
whenever you want.

Chapter 21

WIDER THAN SKY
Just as you love the moon,
you love the stars.
My heart is as wide as the sky.
You forget me
being in trance.
I am a refuge like.
Whom you love
are my refugees.
I don't treat you
as you treat me.
You are wider than the sky.

Chapter22

TRESSES
My heart is
busier than it is.
My nerves and veins
are more oscillating
than earlier.
My body shivers
in a dancing mood.
O, my gal,
what made you push me
into madness?
Just as the waves,
your tresses are
rising and falling from
the black ocean you
hung it loosely on the back.

Chapter23

STORY TELLER
So long as
you are a good
story teller,
I remain a good listener.
The bitterness you
Express it as others
is in fact of yours.
You want to
discourage me
somehow or other.
Ours is the best pair, dear.
Continue your endeavours
without a break.

Chapter24

I write my love story
on the sand.
I know the fact that
the waves wash it out.
I do again and again.
They are wiped off every time.
I repeat this until my errors
are exhausted.
I present myself
before you then
when I am a blank sheet.
Love can't be worded.
It is an erroneous action.

Chapter25

GOD

What can I do, O, my God?
My painful legs pat me
igniting my move still.
My sleepless eyes make
my pain sleep going out
with widening eyes
in her search.
The wind seems left its
promise to winds.
The river seems diluted my hope.
Shall I believe in myself
or in someone else?

Chapter26

UNSPOKEN

Coming, dear.
I heard your
unspoken words.
You need not shout
from miles as
your heart beats
strongly hit me.
I may reach you
as a ray or rain
or as the flowing river
or blowing wind.
Sad, I go unnoticed.
However,
I caress you many times.
I travel from miles.
You need not shout.

Chapter27

BREEZE

Hear a sweet song of breeze.
To you,
a flowing river makes hubbub
but it asks you to
sit on its bank.
Scattering rubies of burning coal
irritate you
but they teach you to shine
until you vanish.
Rain might prevent your move
but it says never stop despite
falling from heights.

Chapter28

CLIMBING UP
Climbing up is
not just as
climbing down.
You are on the top
where you were born.
I'm at its bottom.
Here I start my walk.
I travel half and rest.
Finally reach over there.
Birds whispered your beauty
in my ears all vanish.
I see you droop
in silver hair.
My love has ripened.

Chapter29

TRANCE
My love is
inseparable.
You see me
as a whole.
Me, a drop of rain;
a speck of dust and
a layer of wave.
You know me as
a flood for a drop.
Being unaware
you pick me up and
I fall in trance
on the ground.
With high contentment
I sink and vanish
leaving no trace behind.

Chapter 30

RAY

The ray travels,
the river flows,
the wind blows,
the cloud rains
and the snow falls.
Wherever you are,
my whispers of
love reach you, dear.
You can't escape from me.
If the ray misses you, it
may soon be the river or cloud.

Chapter 31

SKY
When the sky
is cloudy, the shedding
drop is warm
and the lashing
breeze is cool,
I come flying with
the collection of
Nature's fragrance
and take the
throne beside you.
Don't treat me as
tight lipped.
I nest in your lap
until my mouth
is full with the
terms of love.

Chapter32

DAY LIGHT
Pleaded the night
to show me the
day light sooner.
To me. it said
I had to wait and I
waited, tired and slept.
I dreamt a dream
wherein I restlessly
moved in the day light
and slept in the hot Sun.
Light and darkness are
either face of life.
I realized I
couldn't go against them.

Chapter33

IN MIRTH
I am the one
who never runs.
Wherever I am,
I can view the Moon
being a star near or far.
My love is endless
just as the sky and
your smile, just as the earth.
Hold your head up in pride
as the earth does.
The Sky bows
to your smile
forever in mirth.

Chapter34

ATTACK
What a sudden attack!
You are in clouds' disguise
till now.
My paining neck is
looking up to see you rain
and splash the murky souls.
See you brush the sky bluish.
A sudden knock on my door that
at last you melted and rained.
What can I offer you?
No scarce of water now.
Will you have it dear?

Chapter35

CURLING
Me, a curling fog
in winter.
A swaying flower
in spring.
A dancing breeze
in summer.
Allow me to be
a painting brush
in your hand.
It curls, sways,
dances and paints
my lovely heart
to gift you.

Chapter36

GUESS
I guess
a question
that I get
it from you.
My every move
is an answer to you
that keeps you silent.
I am fortunate for
you feel my madness.
It is deathless even
in my absence.

Chapter37

FLY

I fly or run or walk.
Never do I
exceed my line.
Why should I do
when my nest
is her heart.
The souls that
live beyond my limit
pity me excessively.
Their desire needs a palace
whereas their souls lie somewhere.
They treat me as solitary.
What they know about
my spacious nest?

Chapter38

TENSION
Read, dear, read.
I know she
who reads me
frowns her brows.
It's just a pretext.
So, doing, my
attention she draws.
My tension so high
she grows.
I know her
inner soul is otherwise.
Its is a ripened love
unlike the outer's, so raw.

Chapter 39

A LOVE SONG
When the beats
of my heart
sing a love song,
why do my lips move?
When the gestures
of my eyes pour
affection upon you,
why do they shed tears?
When my love has
no words, why/how
do my signs
sign a love note
as yours forever?

Chapter 40

DELIBERATE STRAIN
You carry the pain
on your shoulders.
Heaven doesn't
load it on or
drop it on you.
It's your own gain;
a fruit of your
deliberate strain.
You treat yourself
as a speck but
not as a mountain.
Whom you feel close are
in fact, the distant ones.
For them
you are forever
out of sight.

Chapter41

MASTER
Hey, Master,
don't draw me
so blue.
I am jealousy
of my image,
If it looks
just like me.
I never fly
to near the sky
or I never try
to reach
any ocean as I
don't want
to make them
feel inferior.

Chapter42

HYPERBOLE
Lives move light here.
Pleasures unburden
them but
their toil heavily
loads their eyes
with sleep.
Don't shed salty sweat
to empty an ocean when
your sweat is its
great inflow.
sweat to sleep but
not to weep.

Chapter43

YOU DON'T KNOW ME
You don't know me.
I reach you
as a ray of the sun.
You fulfil your hunger.
I fan you
as a gentle breeze.
You get rid of your sultry.
I caress you
as a rain drop.
You freshen your face.
I hold you firmly
as an earth.
You get mother's love.
Your needs change me.
You don't know me.

Chapter44

A WHITE ELEPHANT
My present craves for
a white elephant that
swims in the clouds.
Me, fly amok like a mad bird.
There,
no dwell to shelter and
no base to rest my feet.
My rumination of past
brings back my geniality
to my memory.
O, God,
bring it back.
I relearn to stand
on my own legs.

Chapter45

CHORE
Charmingly and pleasantly,
I bathe, preen, complete
my chore and be ready
with my clean plumage.
No hurries as my thoughts
take off before I do
and reach you to hug.
Yours and mine
fly far off places and
forget everything
taking in you and me, so sad.

Chapter46

A LOST LOVE

It's a pain of a weak soul.
Being dumb, she can't howl.
Her wilted eyelids speak the tragedy whole.
She is tired of seeking justice.
But, to her misfortune, justice is with a big hole.
She is to change.
Must muster her courage.
Her tragedy be brought onto the stage.
Those who pass justice work on a wage.
Their literacy doesn't make them a sage.
Come on, my weak soul.
Make their dwell forever a hell.
Rest not until they die behind the bars or on the gallows.

Chapter 47

WHAT IS LOVE?
Cut the sleepless nights.
You feel the hunger but you never care.
Is it love to your mind?
To feed her with the fruits of love,
all the sweet words you grind.
The cool breeze irritates you but enjoy the Sunny day's wind.
Adopt the culture of Nature.
The ocean never loves any creature.
A cyclone's is not a venture
as it never needs to do any adventure.
The rain has not any intention to quench your thirst.
The earth harms herself with cracks when it quakes.
The fire spreads and burns all.
Is it its desire to caress all? Not at all.

Chapter48

VENGEANCE
A gentle breeze makes her roll on the ground.
A drizzling makes a rill
momentarily and wet her throat.
Is she alive?
I guess, she is not.
A green lizard springs out of a bush
onto the ground.
A thorn praying to the sun
pierces its throat unintentionally.
My keenness widens its eyes.
The lame ant pays off its
old scores thus and moves away in satisfaction.

Chapter49

BETTER HALF

Your problem is your thought.

You are hurt even by the giggles of a tot.

Might God have forgotten to bless you right?

So bright I am for I am speaking to myself.

Otherwise I face with you surely a fight.

Dear shall I show you a way out?

Strictly be choosy of words before you speak out.

Please spend with a mirror daily.

Fight with the reflection gravely.

Practise a mantra, fight not and gain not foes.

My lap is ready to solace you.

Make it forever your palace.

Let's continue our role as contestants in the race.

Chapter50

ME NOT BUT MY THOUGHTS
I go on my way.
Never do I count the miles
how many I leave behind me.
From home, I am away.
My journey never stops.
My will never drops.
My heart is the Sun.
Always does it burn.
The seeds of my dreams grew well there.
It was a pretty flower garden.
There I was a guard and the garden, my den.
It was burnt by the cold hearted.
Just as the Sun sticks to the east
I stick to my den, a burnt garden.

Chapter51

LOVE

My years of love hidden behind my smiles.

Imagination is my source.

With it along I walk miles.

It is my first gesture

as a child I wore.

You are the strong imprint.

Happily, I bear it.

God's justice made me dumb.

With it along I walk miles.

I say numerous times, "I love you. "

What's the use?

My years of love

hidden behind my smiles.

Chapter52

INNER FLAMES
It is a cold night.
Seemingly so bright.
The love of rising flames
says relax to the rising Sun.
See people for warmth sit
around the fire.
Some sing and some dance.
Thus, time goes on.
My mood is off.
The flames in me keep me awake.
I feel the chilliness.
My spine sways like a tender plant.
I must correct myself.
I need warmth.
No way I must join them.
The love of raising flames
may say relax to my inner flames.

Chapter53

PEACE

A mile a minute,

I move amok, peace to get.

My eyes are keen.

While my heart is searching for it.

Everywhere is unrest.

Farm fields turn to ash.

Jungles to trash.

Man-eaters used to dash man at his threshold.

Forefather's toil

turn the lands into fertile soil.

Sadly, lands in a grey sari now

never be seen wear a sari green.

Blood must boil

until unrest rests in peace.

Chapter54

YOU AND I
Dwell on the verge of horizon.
You are a book of complex terms.
My brain lacks stock of words.
To read you, I have a poor knowledge.
I am not arrogant.
I am not dominant.
I can't blame you as a stone.
I can't praise you as a flower.
I am like a flood that hits you.
albeit you sustain as a stone.
I am like a wild wind that shakes your petals
although your patience flowers.
I know I change.
I know you never change.

Chapter55

GOD

I nod nor shake.

Neither pleasant nor ferocious.

You see a thin rill

between my lips, however

the words never flow.

Yours is an ocean of adversity.

Reach me like a wave.

Make the ocean upside down

as you want to spill out your pains.

You build a mountain of plights.

Be on the top or bottom.

Never makes any difference.

Reach me like a detached boulder from the mountain.

I nod nor shake.

Just learn to float by the flow.

Chapter56

WHO AM I?
On the vast earth,
Who am I?
My dwell is a speck.
I step out and step in in mirth.
Who is it?
If anyone asks my neighbour,
he frowns his brows as if
he did not know me since my birth.
I step out and step in in mirth.
My forefathers did the same until their death.
The world seems today like the Sun.
His is an eye can show you even a speck.
His rays are his love.
They caress all and me too.
I am fortunate
as I know his rays and
he knows my speck.

Chapter57

LOVE AND PEACE
A hollow in our hearts an
empty vessel like it acts.
With the beats of volume high
Our souls it aches.
A low cry of these tiny fishes from the depths of an ocean
reaches the shallows deafening.
Lack of love and peace
magnifies the decibels of sound.
Fill the hallows with it
that makes the smiles reach the shallows.
Beats of our hearts break our dumbness
Singing out the song of love.
No more aches
but only
echoes of peace.
The Sun is our God.
Humanity is our religious book.

Chapter58

This is me.
Never call me a tender one.
Kneel not down as
your care on me
Is just a pretext.
Go, man, go.
Your jungle awaits you,
where you never wilt and can sleep
under the roof of pleasures.
This is me.
Never call me
a tender one.
If the wind is gentle or not;
blows or doesn't; I sway or be still,
I am strong.
Kneel not down
as your care on me
Is just a pretext.
Go man go.
My jungle never awaits you.
Our roof is sky.
Our dwell is the earth.
Age wilts us and we fall.
In the sun'
In the rain and

In the cold alive or dead. We are alike.

This is me.

A flower.

Never call me a tender one. Go man go.

Chapter59

MY DREAM'S REALITY
Only at nights
I know it recurs.
That is why
I fall asleep soon.
A dream, I dream.
My love in a white garb
grabs my glance.
This innocent me
near her almost.
You know my hug is
Just an inch away.
I know I am lucky.
Just a half second sooner
I wake from my dream.
And I miss the hug, so great.
A dream I dream.
A short distance I have to journey yet.
A little later I have to work out to wake.
However, I can't.
I know it keeps my desire afresh.
An inch-long journey and by a half second my sooner wake
Keep me, my love forever pure.

Chapter60

A WATERY DOLL
Hey, my rising doll,
reach me soon.
I am still tall.
Seek the ocean to lift you up.
Ask the winter
to freeze you when you raise.
I am fixed at my place physically.
I can't shorten me. Or at least bow
to caress you.
My rolling doll,
reach me dear. I am still tall.
Just as all, we live
under the sky.
My fractional glimpse of your beauty
make me cut my days downcast.
My raising doll,
seek the ocean to lift you up.
When you surge out of joy
your droplets distract the view of my eyes and
the wind wraps you and hides you from me.
Hey my watery doll in windy attire,
ask the cold to freeze you when you raise tall.

Chapter61

It is your age.
Me, never mock you as
I just overcome that stage,
somehow, after a great struggle.
I guess, at this moment,
You are somewhere
deep in thoughts but physically
a little away from me.
Your eyes say so much
while your mouth shut.
You know, I can read their pulses.
Moving in the balcony to and fro
you make none suspect you that
you are in flight with me.
Often your eyes
See up and sometime as change down.
It is all merely to catch my eye.
I smile but you leave me
frowning your brows as if my gesture disgusted you.
Being in chaos, you tell your
friend's love story in aversion,
Your so-called friend I know
Is your inner soul.
It is your age.
Me, never mock you.

I have just overcome it
after a great deal of struggle.

Chapter62

DIVORCED SOUL.
My pretty soul,
hasten up your move.
Never be too old to realize
that your destination is just beside you.
Always don't look up.
Nothing has its base there.
Or nothing is hung to a hook
that helps fulfil your need.
Don't strain your soul aiming at the vertical paths.
Your anger has made me silence since we became one.
Later, my silence became a cause to your anger.
My heart is your nest.
You need not knock on to
have your entry.
It is widely opened to give you
a red carpet welcome.
Our love has its heirs.
It makes us both equally responsible.
You had better realize it soon,
my pretty soul.
Your destination is just beside you.

Chapter63

MAN AND BIRD

Come on, my chirpy bird.

Don't look at me with fearful eyes.

Don't jump away from me.

More precious than flying is shown.

Come on, my chirpy bird.

I don't monkey about you.

You don't be so fickle with me.

I don't show you grains to trap you.

Sure, you are at gain.

Believe me.

Come on, my chirpy bird.

By words of mouth

we exchange our love.

If I say I love you,

what will you understand?

Believe me.

Come on, my chirpy bird.

More precious avocation than flying is shown.

I will make you learn and

you will make me learn how to express love.

You in words and I in chirps.

Come on my chirpy bird.

to hear me chirp, I love you.

Chapter64

A BEAUTIFUL DWELL
A strange way
I choose is making
a mountain my dwell.
No intervention of man.
It's a narrow pathway.
This highway is full of stones and pebbles.
So, my dwell is not so high.
An opened mouth of a rock,
of course, shelters me.
No wealth I have inside it.
So, I don't need to shut its mouth.
No dampness that irks me.
Rock's opened mouth is my dwell.
The dried twigs are my fuel.
In earthen vessels, I cook that are
made by me.
The burning sticks remind me
the lights
that throw the darkness out.
I go out to snip the bottle,
bitter and ridge gourds.
Some are plenty and some are scarce
which are sown by my pretty birds.
They wish me daily with their chirps in the morning.

Chapter65

The Wood.
Chit---pat
Chit—pat, chit---pat.
While burning,
the wood sings up.
Uff…huff, huff.
The blowing wind adds
Oil to flames.
The curling smoke scatters
and forms a mini sky over.
The slowly raising flames stop a
cat walk and start a dance
in joy.
The huddled birds with cold
circle around over
my head and some boldly
sit around my natural
Stove made of stones
In a triangular form.
The boiling rice skip out
of the vessel and serve the
Breakfast to the birds that
Surround there affectionately.

Chapter66

O, my angel,
unfold my undated letter.
Love is my native place
You receive it,
of course, from there!
O, my angel,
unfold my undated letter.
To get your consent,
my love doesn't crave,
Love is love!
That's it!
My love is singular and
for sure uncountable.
If yours joins it, never does it be
a plural.
I don't call it loves!
O, my angel,
unfold my undated letter.
My yesterday's glance at you
made me a chanter of you.
I don't need your appearance.
For, I myself am your worshipper.
O, my angel,
unfold my undated letter.
my love was born yesterday

and is flying today.
Its tender feathers make
not any noise
and talk not about my love.
You are yet to wear wings.
I will wait, dear.
No matter how long it takes.
Sure, you come flying
and reach me to say
"I love you"
O, my angel,
My letter is fresh
and is evergreen.
Unfold my undated letter.

Chapter67

REST IN PEACE
Is it a fragment of sophistication
that took off bit early
to have its place
beside the stars in the sky?
Have his smiles
hastened up themselves
to beautify the moon
during lunar fortnight?
Before joining the soil,
has he joined the heavenly souls?
My crawling tears on the cheeks
Scribbled so much about him
that my pain alone can read.

Chapter68

VALUE LIGHT
Why am I like I
unlike they?
The swaying flower cheers me,
as a rule, with its soft petals.
I wonder how it knows my tears
are of pain or delight?
I get rid of my shivers
with the showers of rays.
Turns wonder on me how
they know about my weak soul?
Night darkens my day.
How pleasanter it is!
Again, I wonder
how it knows
to make me
value light at dawn.

Chapter69

They don't have any intention
To catch my attention.
I accidentally happened
To see the window stay
Of an abandoned house.
Two living souls,
a pair of pigeons,
started their stay there.
Days trolled by.
I met with them again.
I saw them gather twigs.
as well the blades of grass,
Soft, mushy and slushy ones.
Days rolled by.
I happened to confront them again.
One was constantly
Sitting on the soft mat
which they together made.
I realized she was in calf.
I realized the stay where they stayed
Was not a furnished one.

Chapter 70

NIGHTINGALE
My eyelids drop and droop.
I am so deep in sleep
But my heart is so keen.
It views you in brown.
You walk in the sky
Like a lioness.
Hear you speak to me in roars.
It makes my soul shiver though
It is a dream.
My eyelids drop and droop
I am so deep in sleep
but my heart is so keen.
It views you in too black.
Sad, you are not seen.
Hear you speak to me
in a song, so sweet.
Who are you, dear?

Chapter71

HUMAN
I saw a wooden piece
Float by the river.
It is rising and falling
Being in obedience with
The flow.
If I were in its place,
I thought, I could float
Joyously.
I don't quaff but
I saw a toddy tree
on the bank.
No sooner did the idea
strike my mind than
I reached the tree.
I had two pegs or three.
The wooden piece transmigrated into my soul.
I felt I was lighter than a feather now.
Rising and falling,
I floated by the air and reached home.

Chapter 72

HUES

Hopping with a great hope.
Her eyes are icing my stony heart.
Her needle-like nose is surging her
Beauty and piercing my heart causing no pain.
Her fluttering wings are unfurling the hidden colours.
Her hope came true this way enthralling me.
A dwarf nature flying before my eyes
Painted my thoughts with the universal hues.
Momentarily,
I felt as if I were in nature's lap.

Chapter73

ANIMATE PALACE
My mad love wants to place you in a palace.
My collection of twigs and grass,
dried and dead, makes me build a
typical nest.
It is a lifeless shelter where
I start my life with a ray of hope.
The fluttering leaves around my dwell
blow a trumpet and say to start my war of love.
I battle and I win you.
However, I am lone in my nest but
with you in an animate palace.
Must I disclose it as my heart?

Chapter74

DAY'S DREAM

The day is tired of being thirsty in the sun.
It sheds tears and dripping sweat joins but both
could not make a tiny puddle too.
Thought, night would be a great solace.
The heat waves hit the night and make it wilt.
The clouds give them a big shower.
The day snores the whole night.

Chapter 75

THE WORLD TO BE
I want the world
to send the ray of hope
to every of its corners.
I want the world to have
the blazing desire to extinguish
the flames of war.
I want the world's red-heart
to be a green-light to unfurl
the brotherhood.
I want the world to tread
the path that its conscience builds.

Chapter76

WAR
I don't want the world
To light up the firewood
Under the cooking vessels
with a rocket bomb or so.
I don't want the world to
see the victims sit
near the burnt houses and
wipe their tears of flames.
I don't want the world
to clap its thigh or
trim moustaches
after havoc happens.

Chapter 77

SHAMEFUL DEEDS
I don't do any shameful deeds.
My dirty clothes remind me
my day's toil.
You know, I sigh happily
in the end of the day.
My belly will have
what it wants plentily
with contentment.
My sleep never wakes me up or
never forever sleeps untimely.
The smile I wear
never fades as my clothes do.

Chapter78

LASHING RAIN
The night's rain seems
relaxed by the dawn.
With the songs
of hens I woke up.
My rain-soaked dwell
still struggles to drip the drops.
The dews on the flowers
seem like sweat on my cheeks during my labour.
Perhaps, they too shed it to shield
their beauty from the lashing rain.